National Naval Aviation Museum
The Historic Collection

 Published 2011 • ISBN 978-0-9845636-0-9
Printed in the United States of America

Eugene Ely landing on board the *Pennsylvania* (ACR 4) in January 1911.

Contents

Introduction

Walking amidst the array of aircraft displayed within the National Naval Aviation Museum, visitors cannot help but marvel at the progression of technology symbolized by the winged weapons. Yet, there is a limit to the stories that they can tell, the silence of their deeds mirrored by their engines that no longer roar. As with all of mankind's endeavors, these flying machines are indelibly linked to the humans who built and operated them. These very personal connections come in the form of voices from the past in hastily scribbled letters from distant stations, clothing or equipment linked to sweeping battles that changed the course of history, or perhaps a memento whose significance once resided in the recesses of a serviceman's soul. The historic artifacts presented in this book illustrate the character of naval aviation and serve to honor and memorialize the men and women whose deeds form its enduring story.

Want More Information?

Our web site offers much more information than we can include in this book. This icon (located throughout the book) indicates that our web site contains additional information for that particular subject.

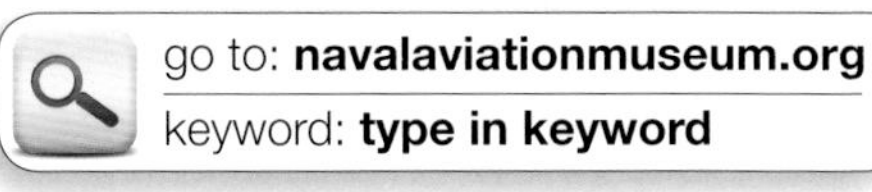

To view the information, go to our web site (navalaviationmuseum.org). From **Exhibits and Collections** on the top menu, click **Search the Collection** in the drop-down menu. Click the **Search** link within the text. Type the desired **Keyword** into the search box and click **Search**. All the information that we have in our database related to your search will appear. We hope you enjoy this closer look into the history of Naval Aviation.

Pre-World War II

The Birth of Naval Aviation

First Fatality

Bent and splintered, this propeller is all that remains of the Wright B-2 aircraft that crashed into the waters of the Chesapeake Bay on June 20, 1913. The details of the crash are noted in a signal message (opposite page, far right). The accident marked naval aviation's first fatality, as Ensign William D. Billingsley fell to his death, and triggered the introduction of equipment standard in naval aircraft since that time—seat belts.

Lieutenant Commander Henry C. Mustin

Naval Aviation's New Home

Letter written by Lieutenant Commander Henry C. Mustin to his wife from Pensacola, Florida shortly after the arrival of the first aviation personnel at the location destined to be called "The Cradle of Naval Aviation."

Mustin

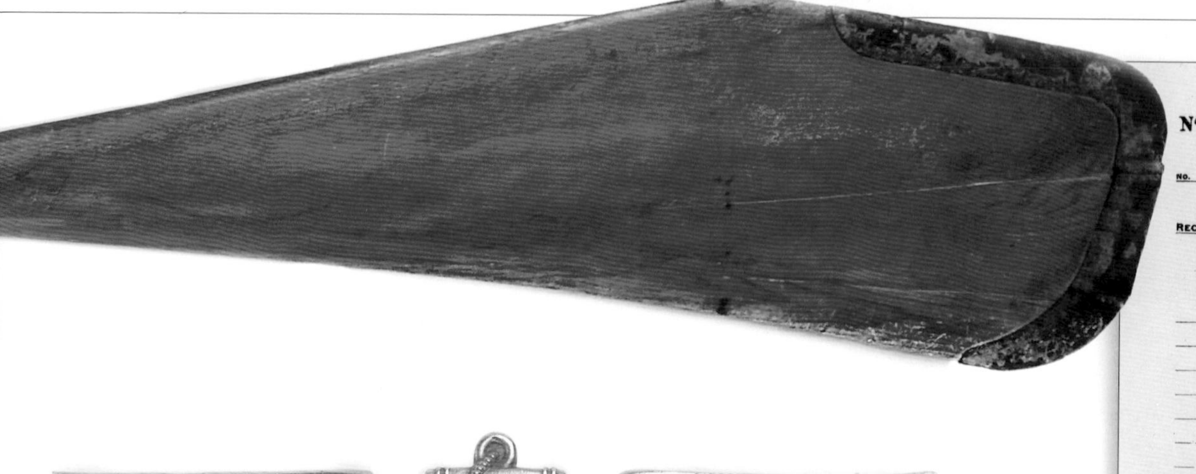

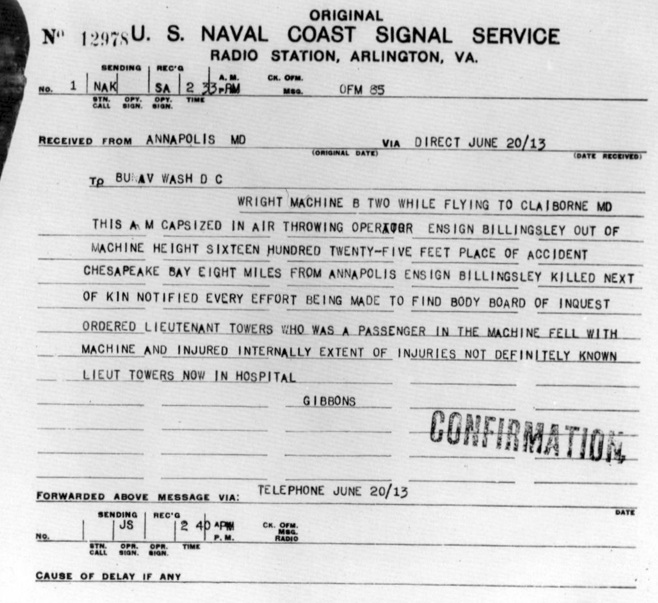

ORIGINAL

N° 12978 U. S. NAVAL COAST SIGNAL SERVICE
RADIO STATION, ARLINGTON, VA.

No. 1 | SENDING: NAK (STN. CALL) | OPY. SIGN. | REC'G: SA (OPY. SIGN.) | TIME: 2 33 P.M. | CK. OFM. MSG. OFM 85

RECEIVED FROM ANNAPOLIS MD (ORIGINAL DATE) VIA DIRECT JUNE 20/13 (DATE RECEIVED)

TO BU AV WASH D C

WRIGHT MACHINE B TWO WHILE FLYING TO CLAIBORNE MD
THIS A M CAPSIZED IN AIR THROWING OPERATOR ENSIGN BILLINGSLEY OUT OF
MACHINE HEIGHT SIXTEEN HUNDRED TWENTY-FIVE FEET PLACE OF ACCIDENT
CHESAPEAKE BAY EIGHT MILES FROM ANNAPOLIS ENSIGN BILLINGSLEY KILLED NEXT
OF KIN NOTIFIED EVERY EFFORT BEING MADE TO FIND BODY BOARD OF INQUEST
ORDERED LIEUTENANT TOWERS WHO WAS A PASSENGER IN THE MACHINE FELL WITH
MACHINE AND INJURED INTERNALLY EXTENT OF INJURIES NOT DEFINITELY KNOWN
LIEUT TOWERS NOW IN HOSPITAL

GIBBONS

CONFIRMATION

FORWARDED ABOVE MESSAGE VIA: TELEPHONE JUNE 20/13 DATE

No. | SENDING: JS (STN. CALL) | OPR. SIGN. | REC'G (OPR. SIGN.) | TIME: 2 40 P.M. | CK. OFM. MSG. RADIO

CAUSE OF DELAY IF ANY

Wings of Gold

Though the first officers began receiving instruction in the art of flying in 1911, not until 1917 did the sea service approve the wings of gold insignia that to this day identifies the wearer as a naval aviator.

This example belonged to Lieutenant Commander Godfrey DeC. Chevalier, who in October 1922 had the distinction of becoming the first man to land an airplane on the flight deck of *Langley* (CV 1), the U.S. Navy's first aircraft carrier.

A Pioneer's Dress Blues

This dress blue tunic belonged to Lieutenant (junior grade) Clarence K. Bronson, a pioneer naval aviator who, like many of his contemporaries, lost his life in the dangerous formative years of naval aviation. Bronson was killed in the premature explosion of an aerial bomb during a flight at the Naval Proving Ground in Indian Head, Maryland, on November 8, 1916.

Vera Cruz Insurrection

Medal of Honor awarded to Commander William A. Moffett for his actions while in command of the cruiser *Chester* (CL 1) during the Vera Cruz Insurrection. Without any clearly defined parameters for the award, more Medals of Honor were awarded to naval personnel at Vera Cruz than in any single military engagement in U.S. history. Vera Cruz was also the scene of the first combat flights of aircraft in U.S. history, missions flown by naval aviators.

The Father of Naval Aviation

Though he once viewed anyone who got into aviation as either crazy or foolish, Captain (later Rear Admiral) William A. Moffett became a convert to the importance of the airplane to the future of the U.S. Navy when he took command of the battleship *Mississippi* (BB 41) (below) in 1919. Under his command, the ship operated for a time with a temporary wooden flight deck that evaluated the operations of wheeled-aircraft at sea. This sword, the engraving on which ironically misspelled Moffett's last name, was presented to him after his detachment by grateful members of the ship's crew. Both the Medal of Honor and the sword shown on these pages can be seen in Moffett's photograph at right.

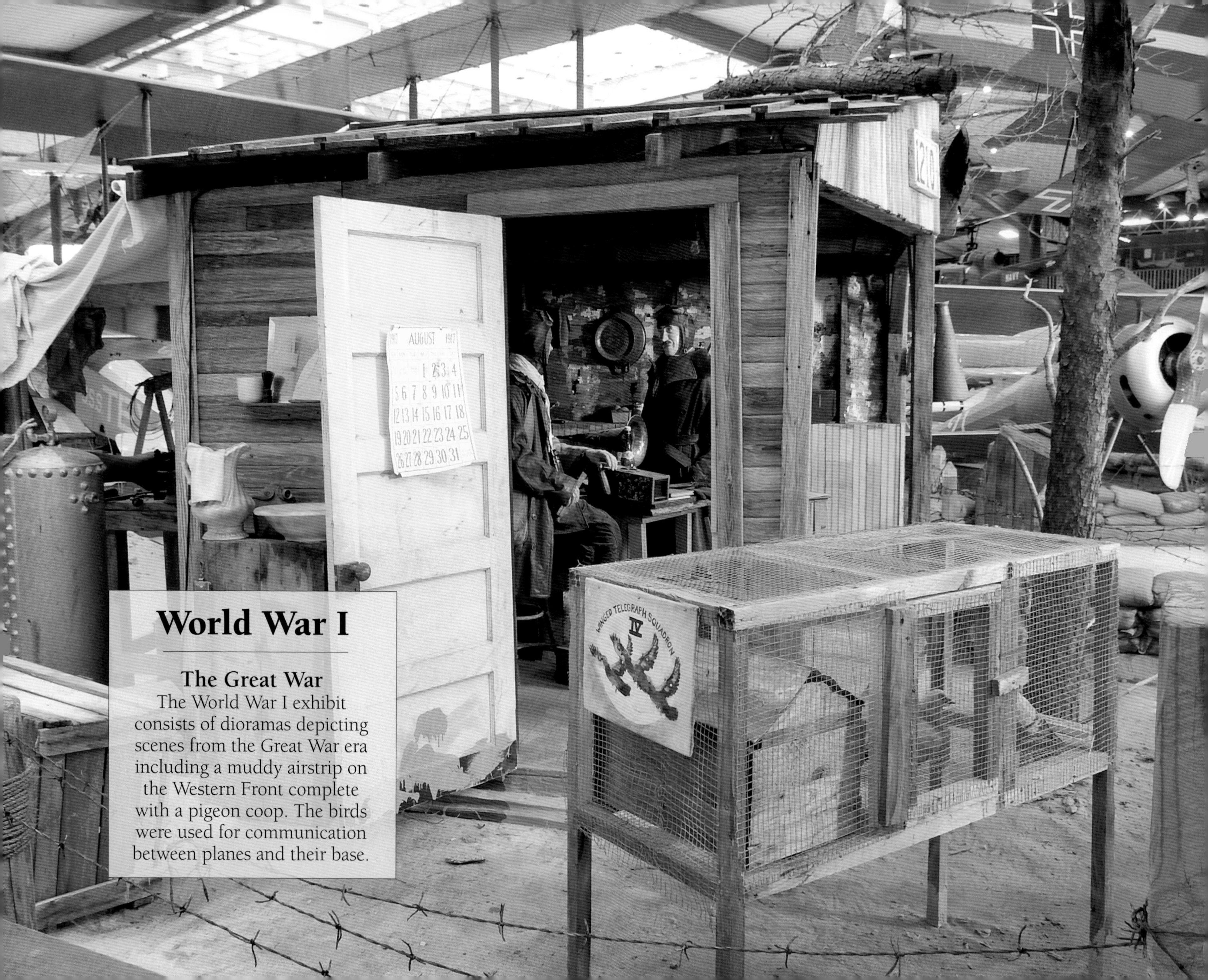

World War I

The Great War

The World War I exhibit consists of dioramas depicting scenes from the Great War era including a muddy airstrip on the Western Front complete with a pigeon coop. The birds were used for communication between planes and their base.

World War I

Cuba 1919

A Sopwith Camel sits on a re-creation of a wooden deck, originally created atop a gun turret of the battleship *Texas* (BB 35) to conduct experiments operating wheeled aircraft in the waters off Guantanamo Bay, Cuba, in 1919.

World War I

The Western Front

A World War I era ambulance—the donor of which actually drove it to the museum—gives the appearance of having slogged through the muddy, trench-filled landscape of the Western Front.